Bar None

CHRISTINE GRIGGS

Bar None
Copyright © 2020 by Christine Griggs

All rights reserved. No part of this publication may be reproduced, distributed, or transmitted in any form or by any means, including photocopying, recording, or other electronic or mechanical methods, without the prior written permission of the author, except in the case of brief quotations embodied in critical reviews and certain other non-commercial uses permitted by copyright law.

Tellwell Talent
www.tellwell.ca

ISBN
978-0-2288-2603-3 (Hardcover)
978-0-2288-2602-6 (Paperback)
978-0-2288-2604-0 (eBook)

Table of Contents

Bar - series 1
Bar Interior 2
Barkeeper 3
Bar Maids 5
Album — series 6
Engagement 8
Skiers 9
Graduation 10
Diana on the Berkshire Downs 11
As You Read This 12
Amenity of the Modern Machine 14
Artist and Model 15
Allegiance 17
A Mote Emotes 19
After the Storm 20
Baby Pictures of Famous Dictators 22
but we will stay 23
Bee On A Snowdrift 24
Best 25
Boston Marathon 2013 27
Buk and Perdy 28
Changing Babies 30

Charcoal on paper	32
Circle	33
Cornish Coastal Road	34
Sparrows' Prayer	35
Slow Hands	36
Sisters Under The Moon	38
River (septet)	40
Sin	41
Pumpkins	42
The Paper Route	44
In Time - Gratefully	45
May/December - The Cold Facts	46
First Grandchild	48
Fecundity	49
Diffidence	50
Death in the Morning	51
Ebb Tide	53
Night Beach	54
Dendrophylax lindenii	55
Dirty Dancing	56
Orientation	57
Past Tense	58
Domestic Bliss	60
Your love song	62
Walter and the Naiad	63
Helpless	66
The Visitor	68
The Blue Book - 1902	69
The Art of Letting Go	71
Winter Solstice (an acrostic)	73
Voluntary Entertainment.	74

Toasted Transgressions	76
The Ghosts Of Storyville	78
The Biographer	80
Whale Station	82
Vancouver, Jan. 2007	84
The Ballad of the Andrea Gail	86
The Blue Note - W 3rd St.	88
The Ballet School	89
The First Bee of Spring	90
Animal Acts	91
Thoughts Served On The Half-Shell	92
Schematic Scapegoat	93
Julius Turing Mourns his Son	94
Fantasy Fruit	96
Letters from the lost	98
Springtime on The Ark	100
Northern Lights	102
Gimme Shelter	104
Erotica at Poetry Night	106
To Be Read Aloud	107
Sinister Christmas	108
Lunatic Love	109
Lost	111

Bar - series

Years ago, in the glory days of Hollywood
when hopes ran high, someone
with more moxie than sense
named it Bar None.

Three neon letters in the center are out
but in this tarnished suburb
of sex shops and hookers it seems appropriate,
no one fixes the B'One.

I'd like to have seen it in its heydays,
tended bar back then but here I am,
in harder times and loving it still.

The parking lot is cracked and weedy,
pock marked by wheels and weather.
I know the sink holes, can drive in blind
and still keep my axels.

Not a welcoming sight, all peeling paint
and rusting beer signs
but it's a fit among the dingy businesses
haunted by skinny Asian girls and their
shabby clients.

In spite of all, my regulars are decent folk,
beaten down but buoyant,
like the place itself.

Bar Interior

It must have been impressive,
luxurious, before smoke and age
reduced it to its present state of
gloomy melancholia,

Only at night by the light from
the bar, filtered through regiments
of amber bottles, does the memory revive.

Fresh smoke covers the stale
and ample bottoms cover the battered stools.
The center of attraction is solid mahogany,
burnished to a glow by a generation of
barkeepers' cloths, eager elbows and
the occasional drink-flushed face.

The floor, seldom seen, is carpeted,
a pattern long gone and the weave
worn thin beneath the stools.
There's a raised area, hardly a stage
but now, with live music a memory,
the only slow-dancers are tables and chairs.

Barkeeper

I know them all,
these dour drinkers;
know their names and ailments,
the hours they keep and what their "usual" is.

I have it ready on the bar
at their customary stool before they
even reach the light,
Chivas-rocks, vodka tonic,
tequila with beer chaser, Margarita extra salt.

They hunch in sullen silence
or whisper sweet nothings to their cradled love
that slowly kills them for their devotion.
It is my lot to be the accomplice,
to watch the slow decline,
the liver spots and bloated hands,
the shakes and, at last, an absence.

Someone always claims the vacancy,
hooking heels over the rungs and elbows
fitting the bar by design. New faces soon get as old
as their stories and still I nod and smile,
wiping, wiping, always wiping.

All night they buy me drinks to make me stay
and listen, elaborately insulted if I decline.
Some mornings I wake alone, fully dressed
with no memory of leaving work
or how I got home.

Bar Maids

They come and go like days of the week,
Some easy to recall
with a prickle of arousal,
others better left undisturbed
in the murky mud of memory.

Hopeful young things from the hinterland
with stars in their eyes, chance call-backs
still a thrill, or out-of-work has-beens
surviving on cat food and a tarnished past.
Occasionally a student of obscure subjects
and one or two professionals, newly jobless,
despairingly directionless

Oh, I had my favourites,
Thelma with her augmented breasts,
the orb unnaturally hard in my palm.
Bonnie, all boney hips and sass,
she could make me come with just a look.
Sweet Jenny, missing sleep as she concocting
the next Cocktail du Jour.
All gone, on to a better life I hope.

Album — series

Weather is not kind to binding
left out
certainly not here
in this back alley,
forgotten by the clean-up crew,
ignored by the dumpster divers.

The snow and rain,
the baking sun,
have had their way.
This ordeal has buckled the leather,
mildew consumes it
gluing leaves together.

Wind turns pages
randomly
with no one to see
or remember the residents.
Posed singly or in groups
stiffly as if the camera threatens,
smiling warily to oblige
"cheese"
teeth bared patiently.

What neglected stories languish?
Fragments fixed
in yellowing linen corners,
grouping the characters
for one final bow.

This is reprieve,
another curtain call,
a glimpse of their stories
woven in these warped pages.

Here is a beach,
here mountains,
now a garden riotous with sepia flowers.
This one in Trafalgar,
timeless pigeons
in permanent mid-air
around the heads of two laughing girls.

Engagement

The undulated edges
date this picture,
older than the page it clings to.

Dress and hair style sometime
between the wars.
Her skirt well below knee,
his pants wide and cuffed,
their shadows long on the grass.

There are just the two,
youthful and shiny with hope.
He holds a pipe
as if hoping to make him
look older.
Her toes point slightly inward,
childlike.

His arm circles her waist,
casually possessive
and she is comfortable,
her altered hand on his,
meeting him half way.

Her unfamiliar ring
catches the early light.

Skiers

Sepia image, snow blankets
the crouching roofs of chalets,
shrinking from the sharper peaks beyond.
Skiers smile cultivated smiles,
ready for the toil to take them
up to powder.
All young, they have a lifetime
to slide smoothly into the future.
No high-tech gear or groomed hills,
theirs is the pioneer route,
original, untrammeled trails
feeling like the end of the earth
in its silence.

Graduation

A fluke has caught
the tossed hats level
above ecstatic smiles
like birds on a wire
waiting to leave
for a better perch.
Below, the gowns
billow with hope
and the winds of
change. Gathered
on the brink they
shimmer with
expectation.

Diana on the Berkshire Downs

This one has colour depicting bright sun
and the wind, whose hand strokes
the distant fields to a paler green
and tosses fair hair in a hurly-burly
blur of curls that she tries in vain to tame.
The distant cushion of the downs
roll away under clouds that mimic the swell
of long dead sea creatures beneath her feet.
Almost hidden by her shadow and the grass,
a red dog, tongue lolling, eyes alert,
looks out at unseen intrigues only he
can scent. I know this girl, this dog, this place,
can hear the curlew above the rustle and bluster.
It is a remembrance stirred by image.

As You Read This

I see you at your breakfast,
toast crumbs on gingham,
empty eggshells gaping,
on your third coffee.
Lazy sun leaning in the window,
you're oblivious of the glory
as you read this.

I see you on the crowded train,
elbows tucked, confined by the glare
of the obesity beside you.
Perhaps it rains,
speed whipping the drops
into frenzied horizontal relays
across the dirty window
as you read this.

I see you in a hotel room
in a distant city.
The bed looks hard,
you and the shabby furniture
sag wearily.
Air conditioner wheezes with the heat
and street rumble seeps in.
You stand in the dingy light
as you read this.

I see you on a beach,
white sand, elbow propped,
distance surf hissing summer bliss.
Children laugh,
you watch as they scamper by,
remembering.
You are smiling
as you read this.

I see you in our hide-away,
your head in my lap.
A hand tangles my hair
the other holds the paper.
Firelight reflects on low beams
and your face,
the paper trembles
as you read this.

Amenity of the Modern Machine

The DVD machine's eager greeting of
"Hello" and then "Goodbye"
as if reluctant to end our time together.

The seat belt warning politely demands
"Please fasten your seat belt"
not wanting to seem overbearing.

The tires under-inflated, the doors not shut?
A gentle voice reminds me, almost
apologetic In its tone.

The bank machine begs
"Please come again" and
my computer pleads
"Are you sure you want to….?"

My GPS has the voice of my choice
so Sean Connery guides me,
unfailingly reassuring,
to my destination.

Even the silently courteous
automatic door seems to bow
as I enter the store.

Artist and Model

She is content to pose
under his varied gaze,
sometimes a coolly critical squint,
sometimes hotly, erotically open.

He seldom touches her,
his hands restless behind the canvas,
although his eyes take in
every curve and angle.

To test him she will casually open
her eyes through a veil of lashes,
her thighs, as if to ease discomfort,
her lips, knowing his eyes are there.

If he is tempted he looks away
only to return to her. now closed
body, languidly naked,
a Da Vinci smile curving his way.

He cannot fathom if it is desire
or wantonness,
if she is nymph to his satyr?
He hides his desire from her
but she knows her power
and reaches out to touch it
as he flinches away.

Tomorrow,
tomorrow he may allow
her hand to settle but, for now he
tortures them both.

Allegiance

We are the front line,
brothers in a bitter war
suffering servitude
to an addictive enemy,
volunteering against our will,
repeatedly.

Signing on
out of desperation,
ignorance or curiosity.
The reckoning recognized
too late for salvation.

Recruits have no leave
nor let-up
from the degradation
and despair.

Our trenches are the alleys,
mean streets and valleys
below blasé towers,
blind eyes turned inward.

Bivouacked in empty lots
beneath highway over- passes,
barely surviving,
we huddle in narcotic nirvana
until the next
unscheduled onslaught.

Our weapon
becomes the enemy
and our savior.
Needy we bind and bleed,
needles falling until next time
the demon calls demanding more
of our undying devotion.

A Mote Emotes

We float in weightless ecstasy, my countrymen and I.
Invisible, we dance unseen until, perhaps, a beam
of cloudless sun unveils our show to the observant eye

This throng will dance in light and air as if locked in a dream
but often tempo ratchets up encouraged by a breeze.
We are not as benevolent as we, at first, may seem

If we can find your mouth and nose a favourite game's to tease,
your nose will run, your eyes will itch and often cry some tears.
We dance our dance inside your nose until we make you sneeze

Some huddle under furniture, if undisturbed, for years
but I prefer to be alone and dance to my own drum.
I whirl, I float in dreamy drifts, unmindful of my peers

But I am not complacent for I know I may succumb
To mop and bucket, duster or voracious vacuum.

After the Storm

Clouds scud above
whirling birds coasting
wildly high, no need for wings.
Below branches dance frantic
leaving remnants of growth to fall,
abandoned and forlorn.

Squalls pass fast, blown sideways
as they go. Waves whipped
to cream roll seamlessly to shore
where shorebirds skitter,
pitter patter, leaving Sanskrit
secrets in the sand.

Leaning into gasping blasts,
we stagger, made ragged by the wind.
Drifts of seaweed pulled from depths
lie tidy, drying row on row
as tide departs reluctantly,
leaving lavish flotsam.
Treasures for the children,
shells deserted by the life it held
in calmer times. Other baubles,
unexpected on our beach,
an orange, perfect as a purchase,
a Barbie doll skinny-dipping
out of depth perhaps.

The dogs have found a smelly prize,
a fish their size, they paw it,
one glazed eye stares skyward.
We deny the dogs their find,
unkindly leashed.
They tug us home once more.

Baby Pictures of Famous Dictators

There are albums, yellowed by the ages,
lovingly amassed, anchored, leafed through
with affection, for the villains their mothers never knew,
naiveté in eyes, later jaundiced as these pages.

They squint in dappled sun or in front of painted stages,
dressed in starchy clothing, only innocence askew,
unfamiliar with the carnage their later life will do
no signs of the perversions or latter insane rages

that tore up states, extinguished races.
Their legacy dread names in children's books,
triumphant tales of their defeat.

And did their mothers mourn those hated faces
clutching childish smiles, remembered looks
or was their fervent prayer for no repeat.

but we will stay

Familiar chill of watery autumn sun as
cool winds stir early fallers at our feet
and drift wood smoke down
from faded blue.

The nights fall early now
with shiver of star shine, cold moon
and rumours of frost.

Wild birds cry in the chill,
high arrows firing south
promising to return in spring
but we will stay and
wait for snowfall
accepting the stark beauty
of silhouettes
against the salmon sky.

Bee On A Snowdrift

Did he wake too soon
or fly too late
here on his icy pillow
of snow with no blanket cover.

His pollen sacs summer laden,
still his wings look
ready for flight, bright
and clear as the day.

He lies as if asleep
peacefully at rest
his honey days over.

Best

In the beginning
she preferred candlelight
or fire glow,
subdued lighting to mask
imagined flaws.

Gently
he taught her that
to see love
with all its imperfections
is as vital,
as the making thereof.

Then she learnt to like
sunlight, in deep grass
by slow rivers,
his hands flowing over her body,
breaching its banks.

In the lazy rumpled bed,
morning sun smoothing the sheets
as he stretched towards her,
seeking her out once more.

And in the night-wrapped garden
to a crickets chorus
where he'd take her on her knees.

Later,
it was best unplanned,
best when he turned to her
unexpectedly, proud, smiling
his familiar smile
and she would be his once more.

Boston Marathon 2013

In the subsequent vacuum
we turned to CNN for answers
and there he is,
standing head and shoulders above
the reporting rabble clustered round him
like apostles hoping for a miracle.

He patiently replied to questions
he'd already answered, his mind
still on the past four hours in surgery
removing shrapnel from six year old legs
and the last shreds of flesh that attached
a twenty year old beauty to her foot.
His weariness was undisguised yet he listened
to request he could not fill.

He was darkly handsome, movie-star material,
but I had tears in my eyes watching
his struggle for composure
as he backed away apologizing
to return to carnage

Now that's all history
and there is progress,
success, finale. But Martin
is still dead, his mother oblivious,
coma-bound and his little sister
still thinks she has two legs.

Buk and Perdy

Bukowski said,

I don't know of any
good living poets,
but there's this
tough som' bitch
way up in Canada
that treads the line.

He's a drinker too, a ruffian,
loves his women
young 'n sassy,
likes 'em hard to handle.
A real wrangler
and gentleman,
we're a couple-a peas.

Met by chance,
mutual admiration then
a decade long friendship, two
poets on the same page.

They're selling our letters
on Amazon now.
Fifty bucks, American,
per used, paperback copy
fer God's sake!
Two self-confessed dirty old men
sharing poetic smut.

A letter from Al always
pulled me out of my
hung-over, blue funk,
less-than-appealing life
and lent some steadiness,
hope and hard-rock wisdom
to the occasion at hand.

Our letters screamed from our
cages, the gambling and booze,
the poetry and painting helped us
to feel free. We slagged other poets
elaborately and often, holding
nothing back. It's all there, if
you've got fifty bucks you
can see for yourselves.

Changing Babies

Letters become words
then, together
they make sense
and, suddenly,
a trip to the mall
is a whole new
adventure.

SALE

REDUCED

NEW ARRIVALS

Dragged past,
eyes on the signs,
mouthing the words
as they form meaning.

In the washroom,
waiting
for his mother,
a ledge with a sign
above it,
slowly he forms the words.

CHANGE TABLE

"What's it for Mummy?"
From behind the door,
to the sound of the flush.
"For changing babies, Sweetie."

And he's glad he isn't
a baby anymore.

Charcoal on paper

Soft grey ash
smeared to a memory of fire
and warmth.
No grit, burnt to finest dust.
Smooth charcoal molded by thumb
or finger to a semblance
of what once was.
It could burn again to finer still,
stretched to spread in liquid languor.

Here are limbs with fleshy finish,
the rounded curve of breast
or a thigh softly smooth and warm
in blacks and grays. Fruit
in subtle bowls lie easy,
never to be eaten. Unclouded skies
of blue are cinereal here
and nature held in somber mourning
still lives on. A boat on
steely waves sails on
into endless silvered sea
to the edge of a pearly world.

Circle

Summer goes up in smoke.
Raspberry canes burn blue
crackling smokeless,
making way for new growth.

Of each clump
one remains, knowing
how it's done
to lead the way
welcoming swarms
of bees in their search
for sweetness.

Each eager visit
brings more until,
as fruit appears, they leave
for other flowers.

Stragglers, angered by
children stealing fruit,
sting if they can
but there's a penalty
to pay, death comes
among the ruby jewels
she worked so diligently
to create.

Cornish Coastal Road

These blackened trees, trunks bent
against the gale, cruelly combed
by wind without end, are
stubborn survivors in this hostile place.

Claws in the starved soil,
seasoned by sea-salt, they fight
suppression by sand and sea.
Cowed by the shifting dunes
that threaten daily to subsume,
yet their tenuous roots dig deep
seeking what little sustenance
and asylum is on offer.

Birds do not perch here
but ride the currents above,
their calls carried inland
where they dilute to nothing.
This track has seen
the smuggler and the siren,
the wreckage and heroics
and now I scuff the sandy soil
as I toil up this final rise.

Sparrows' Prayer

We give thanks for abundant food,
for outdoor tables
and careless eaters.
Thanks, too, for the generosity,
the thoughtfulness of back yard feeders
and little old ladies.
Protect us all from prowling cats,
from bigger birds and windows
that look like open sky.
Grant us the humility to accept
the voice you gave us
and not to rankle
at the song of the robin.

Slow Hands

Kneeling before her
his fingers comb
through her hair revealing
an ear for cool breath and kisses.
He marvels at the pink shell,
the blonde strands
and her flawless skin,
creamy milk.

Her neck yearns towards
his open hands as they travel
over smoothness the slip
and the slide of silk
from sloping shoulders,
eyes sweep the sweet curve
of her breast and a hand
casually brushes a pleading nipple.

He smiles at her slight quiver,
the flutter of lashes
as his hands gentle down to hers
holding them out away.
Her breasts rise and fall,
breathless he leans in to claim
her mouth pressing her softly back
to lie beneath his hovering form.

Her flesh is cool in his heat,
smooth on his rough.
His hands flow down
the length of her sides
to the swell of her hips.
He inhales her scent.

With his slow hands he opens
the pages of her passion to read
a moment of stillness, tense quiet,
until he finds her centre
and anchors her with a shared sigh.

Sisters Under The Moon

Dear Sister,
this moon, pocked like Sameer's cheek,
floating in the shallow sky
must shine in your eyes too.

I miss you so and hold
your letter against my heart
inside my churidar.

Even though his hair is white
my husband is a kind man
and will not hit me
as Kamna's does.

She says he tells her
her name means desire
and he is afraid
of her beauty so he beats her
most nights before
he takes her to his bed.
Our father chose a good man
to be my husband.

I think often of the village.
Here there is too much concrete
and trees grow in only one place
inside iron railings where people
may sit on wooden seats
to watch them growing.

There is no peace, even at midnight
the traffic drones and sirens,
like the earthquake warning,
howl in the streets.

You beg to join me but
it would be punishment.
London is not a happy place.

River (septet)

In summers' torrid heat, sinuous and slow,
reaching for uncertain future far below
the mountain cascade feeding gnawing need
is just a distant memory of greed
tranquility conceals the winter race
that tore at banks and washed without a trace
last summers detritus in chaotic chase.

But now at ease and slow 'neath shading trees,
the weeping willow boughs that dip and tease
catching boaters passing by them unawares
and pristine swans with wings that whisper prayers.
I have let her hold me in her cool embrace
and teach me life at a much slower pace,
I've found her secrets and her hidden face.

The summer river dawdles to the sea
reaching at last her constant destiny,
a brackish welcome is her final prize
as swirling seagulls greet with raucous cries.
She feels once more the parting salmons' fins
while miles away a mountain spring begins
the race to lowlands no one ever wins.

Sin

He whispers heat and
delicious sin. Suggests
transgressions through
the night as our bodies
meet halfway to heaven.

He kisses my smile
still questioning his
intentions, his fingers
follow tender trails
that find me fighting
for a my breath.

We murmur
of fine wines,
lush sweetness
and velvet ropes.
He whets my weaknesses,
feeds my greed
until I yearn
to own his reality.

Pumpkins

Suddenly, in September
they flood the produce aisles
spilling sunlight
into dingy corners.

Plump progeny
of yellow trumpet-flowers
and hot summer days
when drunken bees droned off
heavy with pollen.

Dotting fields among the tendrils
and heart shaped leaves they shine
waiting to be collected,
heaped onto trucks
that spill them into piles
of orange promise.

We sift the hoard looking for
an impeccable one
to proudly grace our porch
or make the perfect pie,

At home they give up
their slippery seeds
reluctantly in webby clumps
of pumpkin posterity.

They grin bravely
through candle-lit triangle-eyes
and gap-toothed mouths
as if they know the end is near
and glory will be fleeting.

It saddens me
to see the forsaken ones,
stillborn Jack-o-lanterns
lying in scattered piles
imploding slowly
like forlorn orange balloons.

The Paper Route

Waking to dark
this winter morning
careful not to wake the sleeping house,
he eats toast as he dresses for cold
and loads the bulk of paper
into the canvas bag

Once outside the seed of fear
settles in his throat
and he swallows it
as his boots ring out on the frosted road,

Twelve, on the threshold
of manhood, he's proud of this first
responsibility but dogs still scare him
even if a door is between them,
the way it growls at his timid intrusion.
The bag is lighter now but not the sky
and he pauses a moment for courage
knowing it is waiting.

In Time - Gratefully

My legs remember when
and my face still smiles
at the memory.

My hands will hold the feel
of tiny stitches and
that little clasp at the back
of my neck, the hooks and eyes
and troublesome buttons,
of minute brush strokes
and folded paper.

My feet still dance me
fast and loose,
leap fearlessly
from rock to slippery rock
and run to catch the bus,
in my dreams
my knees will cross
in elegance.

May/December – The Cold Facts

She likes my grey-flecked temples
and my condom size,
the fact that I'm experienced
and sexually wise
but with wisdom comes reality,
a certain cruel truth,
the fact that I'm much older
and the fickleness of youth.

I buy her bits and pieces,
the niceties of life
but sometimes she repays me
with such a subtle knife
that cuts me to the quick
and brings me to my knees.
She never leaves with thank you
and often starts with please.

Her appetite's voracious
for anything that shines,
it doesn't take a genius
to read between the lines
but the sex is so fantastic
and the bullet hard to bite.

So I'll be her sugar-daddy
while things are black and white
and when she loses interest
there's plenty more out there,
young things wanting older men
with lots of cash to spare.

First Grandchild

He hadn't noticed, didn't feel –
when did he get so old?
Blinded by ambition,
he didn't see his children grow
or notice them fledge.
Now,
unexpectedly shy he bends to look,
adjusting his bi-focals.

Unblemished eyes gaze into his
with innocence he wishes for.
Fingers, small and untried
with nails like new-born shells
curl round his antique thumb.

Still for a moment
wondering at the unfamiliar,
then finds other brighter shapes
in this intriguing world.

"Hold her, Dad. She won't break."

Oh! But she might.

Too precious,
too fragile to face the dragons that wait.
He vows to protect this tiny life
with his well used one.

Fecundity

First the sighs,
the seething sap.
Burgeoning buds unfurl to sun
flooding the world with
sudden green.

Boughs reach for redemption
after winter's wrath,
wrap themselves
in fresh and feathery habits.

Some buds bundled still,
bide their time
dreaming of glories to come,
the attention of hummingbird,
butterfly and bee

Later when petals spread colour
singing with new passion,
vines twine in tangled abandon.
Flowers droop pollen laden
and dewed with nectar.

Perfumes spice the humid air
and fruit forms
legacy of kisses bestowed
all summer long by drowsy bees
searching out the hidden places.

Diffidence

Where will I take this poem?
To a dusty drawer of whispering older sisters,
a leather-bound book
with tiny lock and
gilt-edged pages or
to your unenthusiastic ear?

If I read it will you hear
and understand
or will I seem obtuse,
a stranger to you?

Perhaps the words will languish,
shallow-breathing,
in the dark until
the paper yellows and the words fade
to silence.

I guard it in my heart
deciding not to share
and for a moment I ache.

Death in the Morning

I killed an ant just now,
solitary and black.
Unaware of imminent death,
doing no harm on a busy
reconnaissance
for a food to take home
but I know when the word
gets out and the trail is set
an army will arrive.

I've done battle with ants before,
big, skittering, black wood ants
under the cabinets,
microscopic sugar ants in the larder.
I admire them all,
their industry and tenacity
but we cannot abide in the same abode.

I only kill
to prevent the messenger
returning home,
spreading the news of bounty,
leading the tribe to the promised land,

It is a quick finale,
painless I hope,
better than a writhing,
insecticidal death

So, sorry little ant,
you were only doing your duty
but so was I.

Ebb Tide

The tide is so low
rocks drowned all year
are sweating dry and you
look the other way
as if it could be
your fault the seaweed's
drying in a haze of stink
no smile
no talk
in fact no sound except for
the whisper of water
on newly found sand
and the crack of drying kelp
under our feet on the edge
of the world a ship
like hope in full sail comes
or goes we neither know
nor care and it silently slips off
the sea lip and disappears
say something
nothing
so we get up
and leave the tide
to cover the stench
of silence.

Night Beach

Through mists
of the discarded day
the moon rises from her sea bed.

Alien world with
ghost lakes and mountains
clear outlined.

So close, she draws us in.

The sand exhales warmth saved,
sun for our naked soles.

Our fleeting footprints fading
as we pass.

Our steps create
fluorescent memories
in the discarded kelp
at our feet.

Warm spray from waves
we only hear,
soft kissing whispers of exotic lands.

Distant thunder,
recalling empty shells
collected
by children with sandy knees.

Dendrophylax lindenii

The Ghost Orchid

Elusive as any ghost will be,
undistinguished until
delicate white blooms
seem to float on air
in the gloom.

Men have died in the
fruitless pursuit to own her
but, if captured
she escapes in death,
refusing to be a
possession.

Fine seeds wafted
on warm winds
found Florida, settled.

Growing to glow in the dark depth
of steamy swamps. Stuff
of legend and inspiration,
pale sister to her riotous
siblings she remains
wildly untouchable.

Dirty Dancing

A hot wind
dances dust
one, two, three
and swirls it
in a dervish spiral.

A capricious partner,
it skips away to snag
a cheap candy wrapper,
yesterdays Gazette
or flirty food-court container.

The fickle breeze
drops them and
they lie breathless
in the gutter waiting
for the next blustery gust
to whisk them off
to dance once more.

Orientation

A familiar route taken
by night or, unexpectedly,
in daylight. Drawn out
before me, welcoming,
endemic but always new.

I will not hurry through
this valley, the moist
meridian shifting beneath.

Coordinates guide me
to a certain center as,
with closed eyes, I feel
my way across plains
smoothed and stilled
by expectation.

There are secret places
here that only you and I
explore, cul-de-sacs and
narrows to slip into and
hide. Scent of sea and,
on my tongue the same
sweet salt.

Past Tense

On an anonymous street
in an ancient town
built below university walls,
a book store is open
at unusual hours.

Full of youthful browsers,
it was our haunt for years.
No new print pheromone
or stacked successes here,
no glossy paper protection
just the musty intrigue
of dignified, if faded, volumes
foxed by previous hands,
red rot halted just in time
for covers bowed by age.

Much thumbed, well read
volumes of classical thought
that open unbidden at a certain page
or reveal spidery comments
in the margin. Once a letter fell,
flattened by years of bondage-by-book,
fine copperplate told of
love and forgotten promises.

Made multifaceted
by their history
these beautiful ruins have more to tell
than all the words inside.

Domestic Bliss

By day she cooked and cleaned,
made a home, He toiled
in the halls of high finance,
pin-striped position of power
and responsibility. An immaculate,
modern couple.

But

at night the front door key
triggered his erection.
She would greet him all in leather,
or naked but for thigh-high boots,
once bespectacled with a metal rule
that left his balls stinging for a week.
Always he'd rise to
her domination.

His dinner waiting
in a dog's bowl under the table,
she'd kick him if he used his hands.

Bad dog!

On good nights she'd find
a reason to flog him and
he would come to their bed
a burning, pulsing nerve where
she'd tease and deny until he
ached for release but she never
let him sleep before
mutual satisfaction.

Your love song

Yesterday
> I wrote you a love song but
> you laughed so
I tossed it in a dumpster.

Today
> I saw a pan-handler
> begging
on the corner.

He was singing your song.
> His hat
was full of hearts.

Walter and the Naiad

His lonely walk takes effort,
oppressive heat,
no shade or breeze.
Doctor's orders, still he rebels.
About to turn back
he glances over the lake,
he is no voyeur,
cannot pull his eyes away
but leans on his cane
afraid to blink.

Breathtaking,
pale against dark ripples,
she bends, splashes a hand
as she wades. Water consumes her,
knees,
thighs
and, as it laps at her buttocks
she turns to reveal a dark triangle
and chill-sharpened nipples.
Eyes blissfully closed she falls

backwards, submerging
then surfacing, her hair slick.
He realizes she is unaware
of an audience, aches to join
her in cool youth.

Seconds it seems, he is naked too,
knee deep, then at her side
in a lazy crawl
he hasn't done for years.
She smiles, unsurprised.
Swims beside him
easily.

"I hoped you'd join me."
"You saw me then?"
"No I felt your presence,
your need." She dives.
He gasps
as her lips find him,
a sucking sea-thing.
He is sinking,
dreaming, swimming gill-like above her.
They break in turmoil
both breathless,
he hasn't felt this way,
perhaps for ever.

His hand explores, a thick,
throbbing dowel grows
from his groin.
Her hand is there,
guiding him, warmth gloves him
in sweet softness as her legs wrap him.
He bucks her mulishly,
every muscle, joint
and part working as it should,
as it could in younger years.

They swim and float as one,
he rooted in her,
she nurtures his desire until,
with a howl of submission,
his release echoes over still waters.

She sinks now,
below and away,
he can see her smile
so clear is the water,
until she twists
fish-like and is gone.

Helpless

There are four beds here,
the fourth is pristine
waiting for weight.

All of us helpless,
watching the days' march,
the nights pass
slowly resigned to swallowing
what is served,
accepting all indignities.

Across the antiseptic divide
lies a stranger
I have grown to love.

Her hair is long and gray,
her body wasted and rebellious.
She is unconsciously abandoned,
restlessly active
in the snowy field, she swims
in her coma.

Today she has soiled herself
and we cannot look
as she rolls in her own filth.
The staff flits frantically past
the open door too busy to care,
unaware of this uncomplaining soul

A tall distinguished man appears,
other-worldly in his business suit,
graying temples.
Assumptions are made,
now a nurse will come
but he is no doctor

A son who stands
for a moment
at his mother's bedside
taking in what she has become
then sadly draws the curtain.

The Visitor

She's at the window wondering
if she got dressed up
for nothing, that he won't be here
to see her new burgundy dress
and jacket with the sailor's collar.

Close to her ear the curtain
sounds like the sea and feels
like comfort.
She fights the urge
to put her thumb in her mouth
for even one second
in case he comes.

Outside the window
Rue de la Paget unfolds
beneath her but she's looking
at me across the street,
solemn and still.
She doesn't return my wave
or leave the window
just in case he does come today.

The Blue Book - 1902

Bellocq

Oh yes!
Tom Anderson,
they called him "King of Storyville."
He had a book, you know,
he published every year.
It was blue, I remember,
with lists and lists of girls.
Alphabetical.
Every single working girl in Storyville
was there, white ones,
black ones,
even pages of mulattos.

When one was killed
or couldn't work for the clap,
he had marks to show the sick
and a neat line through the dead
just so you'd know.
He listed their specialties too.

Olivia the Oyster Dancer could shimmy an oyster
all the way
down
her naked body
from her forehead to her foot
and back.

French Emma would refund
your two bucks
if you held your cum
for one full minute after penetration.
She seldom had to,
so they say.

Then there was Grace Hayes
with her pet raccoon that picked pockets
like a pro.

They don't come like that
any more.

The Art of Letting Go

Cards must be held close
concealing the hand.

It is not to be shared or
communicated.
It is a strength,
one
of a dwindling few.

Abandoned loves lie
discarded,
my progress
of freedom in motion,
the joy
of taking the stairs
two at a time.

The love
of growing things,
close to the earth,
hands deep as roots.

The tenderness
bestowed on
still life,
the commonplace,
gone
yet remain

as memories to visit
in living colour dreams.

Each day a fragment
of life falls away
an ability,
a talent,
a satisfaction,
an ace becomes an ache.

Winter Solstice (an acrostic)

Withered stalks of summer's fruits
incline under cleansing snow,
new shoots stirring even now.
The river groans,
encased in shrieking ice,
reaches for warm seas.

Shamash appears for scant hours
only to sink back, spellbound once more.
Leaden skies belly down
sharing gray with river reflections.
Too-late geese nuzzle brittle crust
in search of food for the next flight
conscious only of an absence,
each one scanning the skies for company.

Voluntary Entertainment.

In the routine grind of aging
Fridays are the high point
of the week at The Rest Home
and it is Christmas week.

Thinning hair combed carefully
across balding skulls, even ties appear
loosely knotted at wrinkled throats,
ancient lipstick shakily applied
and perfume liberally sprayed.

But this kid has made no effort,
his bony knees peer boldly
through torn jeans and his battered
guitar case offers little promise.

Old man Parker grumbles, "Kids these days"
but smiling Mr. Imrie gets a laugh with,
"now we got the drugs and rock 'n roll,
but where's the sex?"

Mrs. Macmillan doesn't raise her chin
from her chest or open her eyes
even through grudging applause
prompted by the kindly staff.

The boy strums chords,
avoiding eyes, as his nervous fingers
find the tune and his confidence grows,
quieting the chatter.

Over the first soft notes
of "Hark the Herald Angels"
rises a thin pure voice,
Mrs Mac has raised her head,
bright eyed and smiling,
remembering.

Toasted Transgressions

Here's to the words said in anger
too late to be swallowed again
and here's to the face turned away
ignoring the person in pain

Here's to the letters not written,
the 'phone calls delayed 'til too late,
raise a glass to procrastination
and clink to that somnolent state.

A salute to my clear imperfections
and a swig to your goals unfulfilled,
let's drink to our everyday failures
and insults too easily spilled.

Here's to the lovers we've lost
so carelessly squandered away,
let's toast all those wasted ambitions,
who cares at the end of the day?

Here's mud in your eye dear old friend,
a toast to those bridges we've burnt,
the regrets we may have that still haunt us,
the Sisyphean lesson not learnt

And cheers to all our shortcomings
To every unreachable door
We'll rejoice in our foibles and missteps
'til there's no more whiskey to pour.

The Ghosts Of Storyville

They're lurking
at Liberty and First.
where the hiss and slap of Buddy's strop
drifts out from the open door
of "N. Joseph's Shaving Parlour."
and the barbers pole still squeaks.

Buddy Bolden's Blues
that Morton wrote before
he blew town
spice the air
still not making much sense.

You might find Bunk Johnson
with Bechet and Pops.
Satchmo' smiling his toothy grin,
wiping it off again,
his hanky stark
against his big, black face;
he and Batch never were on
friendly terms.

So many souls hang out here
waiting for a blow,
lining up in ghostly queues.
Kid Ory telling his story
in Creole,
Bechet treats it gentle,
always understated
like any ghost should be.

The Biographer

By now I know my way
through this holy hospice
and yet a shrouded sister
insists, gliding silently ahead
and my feet, suddenly clumsy
on the stone floor, follow.

Rain christens the
saintly windows
of her white room.

She seems to sleep,
arms above the blankets,
narrow hands resting
palms down like two halves
of a prayer parted by doubt.

I am back once more to prompt
her memories and write
her long life in shorthand.
Later a book
before her illness wins.

Beside the bed, a photograph,
a radiant young woman.
It is she before the years
of heartache.

But now, her Easter Island face
lies in repose, scanning
her remarkable life from behind
her blue veined eyelids.

The old eyes open
sparking a smile of recognition.
"Where were we?

Whale Station

This is an unhappy place,
specters from a brutal time
stalk the stony shores.
Nature has tried to heal the wounds
with saplings and vine while the Sitka spruce trees
stride away from the memories
into damp darkness.

Only stone stands firm,
here a flight of mossy steps to nowhere,
there sea weedy pillars supporting
nothing more than birds
where slip-way or haul-up once waited
for the flenchers and the lacerated giants to arrive.

Foundations and broken walls are just traces
of bunkhouse, rendering shed or bone crusher.
Wood has rotted to a feeling,
ghostly broken shapes worn to the core
by weather and time.
Iron hulks lie here too, rusted red,
memories of the blood spilt. On my hands
it smells of death, geologic,
ancient.

I long to leave this haunted place
and yet it holds me here
in the sun and seabird cries.
Out to the placid sea, away from the sadness
a smooth, dark back arches
out of the dappled swell
sighing sanctuary once more.

Vancouver, Jan. 2007

Hurricane-force in this gentle place,
great cedars lost their grip
held in history.
Pines left standing clenched their roots
bent in prayer for patronage
only to snap at the knees,
left to lie, giant toothpicks,
strewn across the park.

Skies scoured of clouds
dry-eyed and crystal clear.
Stars skimmed the wicked waves
that slap-dashed over battened boats
shattered in the strain
against their maritime bonds
in an unsafe harbour.

Houses shook beneath
threatening trees
protectors only yesterday,
tossed in epileptic agony,
groaned and fell exhausted
on lives below.

Boreas' deafening fury
left mortals shaken
by nature's massive tantrum
and the familiar made strange.
All will revive but
perhaps we sleep too long.

The Ballad of the Andrea Gail

She was no beauty, was this boat,
No oars nor billowed sail,
A working girl with hardened crew.
She was the Andrea Gail.

She started out from Marblehead
Set sail for Flemish Cap
The fishing lacked what they required
And so they called a wrap.

The captain radioed to land
"We're heading back to port"
The seas were angry, waves were high
And tossed the Gail in sport.

They weren't to know this weather would
Be called The Perfect Storm
They'd been through worse than this one was
And they were dry and warm

The troughs were low and tunnel-like
And oft her bows were smashed
Diminished by this fearsome storm
The tempest howled the lightening flashed

The waves grew to a hundred feet
Or more, the darkness shrieked
They rose then free-fell shuddering
The deck and rigging creaked

What wasn't stowed went overboard
The galley was a wreck
The crew fought hard to save their lives
And just to stay on deck

"She's comin' on, boys, comin' strong!"
Was all Captain Tyne's said
The ship and crew were never found
All six men were presumed dead

Each left behind a family,
Acquaintances and friends
Folk heroes now, they still
Live on, a tale that never ends.

The crew - Captain Billy Tyne, Bobby Shatford, Dale Murphy, David Sullivan, Michael Moran and Alfred Pierre

The Blue Note - W 3rd St

A twelve steps shuffle-down
from neon heaven
into smoky darkness
gets you a buzz and jazz.

The news is out,
we have our licence now
you can lace your java legally.

It's homage night to
Mulligan and Baker,
the worshipful crowd won't dance.
Standing room
only the ears have the floor
tonight.

By midnight lips go
cracking notes and no joke
but still they play like pros
and we stay
even though we have
to be up early
while the band sleeps.

The Ballet School

From arabesque to plié,
pirouette to entrechat,
slender necks bend
too short for swans'
but graceful
in their subtlety.

Eyes focused inward,
concentrating,
mouths counting silently
quatre, battement tendu et –
cinque.

The reflected barre mirrors
the pain of years,
the work and ruined feet
forced to bear lightness
on the head of a pin.
Degas cygnets yet to earn
their plumage of white

The First Bee of Spring

Was he the chosen one
to leave the hive,
test the air,
set the course?

Returning with peculiar maps
of nectar itinerary,
decoded for his brothers
in a spastic shimmy.
A bee-line to blossoms
startled open by reflected heat,
azalea and iris,
jonquil and crocus.

Perhaps the sun woke him
from his honeyed sleep,
brisk and eager
before the summer drowse.

Was his effort worth
the early rise
or are the blooms still hiding,
hoarding pollen
for a later date?

Animal Acts

Grovel, waddle, wallow, groan,
Mingle, muster, bluster, moan,
Whistle, bristle, bark and whine
Wiggle, waggle, toot and twine,
Rustle, bustle, wrestle, bleat,
Hover, huddle, coo and tweet,
Slinking, spinning, squawk and squeak
Mumble, mutter, moo and shriek,
Howling, prowling, growl mystique,
Un-translated human speak.

Thoughts Served On The Half-Shell

Now I know the reality of the other half,
the true colour of your eyes and size
of your heart as you fabricate
unblinkingly.

It is a gritty torment to guard
this shard inside
but the hope that a pearl
of truth may form is ever there.

To pry it free before its time would sear
the fine veneer,
curl the mother of pearl from its shell
and reveal an abandoned little well
of hopelessness

Schematic Scapegoat

treading taut on razor wire
tongue of a gazelle
seeking thorny food
arms out for balance
eyes squeezed shut to avoid
the inevitable tumble from grace
you are the seer of lies
talker of truths
the reflective face of faults
you will take our sins
our perception of wrongs
and absolve us
you make banquets
of hats and crow
bouquets of blame and
pilloried wreathes to place
on our monumental mistakes

Julius Turing Mourns his Son

Sharp as a tack, even as a child.
reports reached his mother and I
in India from his schools back home
and later, at Cambridge he seemed to find
a certain freedom.

our beautiful boy,
our brilliant gift,
our monstrous one is dead.

Might as well have been hounded,
Frankenstein-like with pitchfork
and flame, bright wounds
searing the night, but it was words,
an obscene choice in broad day
that drove him on to desperation.
Their nescience, an echo
of the secrets which haunted him.

He died too soon,
too sad,
too unfinished.

Ethel, in her grief,
refused to believe he had died
by his own hand,
calculated,
purposeful.

After all the strife in his work
and life, they cut him loose,
tossed him away,
unmindful that he saved the day
working through a labyrinth,
slipping in the missing piece,
defeating Enigma.

One could say
he died for England
after all.

Fantasy Fruit

On these long, grey days
when sun is a rare treat
my mind is on the sensual,
the unobtainable.
The sinking of teeth into plumpness
that is cherry, peach, berry.
Unbridled rivers of juice,
saliva, lips stained
as if bruised by the indulgence.
Unashamed gluttony savours
the all-too short harvest.
Seeking colour hidden in leafy veils.
Handfuls of plump, sun-warmed flesh.

Inside the snowed-in Supa Store
irresistible banks of temptation
beckon from the produce aisle.
cherries from China, peaches
from Panama, Mexican mangoes
all shadows of what they once were.

Travel worn, miles from home,
they aim to please,
no fault is theirs
that their juice has dried,
their skin coarsened,
their taste graceless,
all left on some freight plane
over the ocean.

And so I return
to my dreams of heat and sweetness,
of U-pic and farmers' markets
fragrant with the summer morning's labour
and wait for the sun's return.

Letters from the lost

From Jewish parents
in Sudetenland fleeing to Prague,
then on to Holland hoping
the children will know.
From learned professors
and kind doctors
struggling to survive
in a crumbling Cambodia.

They flutter
in the mind's eye,
unread,
and undead.

From the private
in the trenches of a dozen wars,
the sailor on a thousand
vessels destined to die.

Last thoughts,
last loves,
last words some notorious,
some unaccredited,
most desperate.

From prison cells,
a final home,
from hospices
and empty rooms,
sealed and stamped,
they pile up behind the doors
of our imagination.

Springtime on The Ark

Even though the skies still weep
and no land's in sight,
no plum blossom or pussy willow,
it's springtime on the Ark.
Animal partners behaving as naturally
as confines allow.

Motion sickness to morning sickness
and Noah places buckets
in strategic spots like ashtrays,
worrying all the while, as bellies swell,
if the Ark can stand the strain

Ham and Japheth, sleeves rolled,
taking turns to watch
for problems, breach births
or other such un-pleasantries.
Mrs. Noah muses, thanking God
it isn't her lying in the straw,
belly tight as a drum.
Catching Noah's eye,
she blushes, blows a kiss.

The Ark is filled with nursery sounds,
bleats and mews and chirps.
As mothers nurse,
fathers preen oblivious
to the repopulating
of a drowned earth.
Above, on deck Noah scans the heavy skies
for his dove.

Northern Lights

He lifts the boy to sit
on his knee. Uneasy
with small children it reassures him
to know his mother is close
to reclaim her son.

He's surprised when the small hand
takes his, the warm, unsullied skin
against his raddled parchment as
he turns pages of an ancient book
of memories.
When the child speaks
his breathe smells faintly
of peppermint toothpaste,
his hair still damp
from the nightly bath.

Tonight the book tells of
The North where the old man
spent his youth, the long
winters where a shy sun
slid along the horizon
and the dreamless night
seemed endless.

Here are pictures taken
years ago of snowy owls
with strangely human eyes,
Arctic foxes and ermine
their splendid fur trapped
only by a lens.

The old man tells of countless
shades of blue. "…and you thought
snow was white? On certain nights
we'd hear a whisper, a low roar
many miles away and outside
celestial alchemy filled the heavens
with great waves of colour"

The small head turns,
his eyes blue questions.
"The Aurora Borealis, once you see it
out there in the crystal night
you're never the same.
One day you'll look up
and you'll see the solar wind blow
a rainbow across the sky too."

Gimme Shelter

The palette beside mine
is too close, the dude mumbles
in his sleep between snores.
The mattresses under me is
thin but it's warm and dry
and softer'n any sidewalk
or park bench.

We're all men,
all colours from
all walks of life and
all in need of sanctuary
of one kind or another.

Each shelter is different,
different rules,
different welcomes and
different cliental.
Some allow pets,
some the carts fellahs use,
some serve food –
those have line-ups
round the block starting to snake
hours before feedin' time.

Mostly it's sullen silence,
men wrapped in worry or
hung-over with no desire
to share. Other nights chat
starts up, hard-life stories
from the fallen high-fliers
or anecdotes that gets us all
guffawin' like seals. Those
are the good times until dark
brings sleep along with the
dreams, seldom sweet.

Erotica at Poetry Night

Isolated in the circling light,
bow-tied and be-cardiganed,
he consults his notes,
mops his brow
and peers out blindly.
"Now?"
Tentative applause,
perhaps encouragement is unwise,
dangerous even, but he is off,
eyes unfocused, toes curling.
"Sir Ego Libido" someone whispers,
a little too loud to giggling response,
if he hears he doesn't miss a beat.
Using words we never knew
could sound this way,
they silence us at once,
make us close our eyes for visions
none of us care to share.

To Be Read Aloud

Prattle, rattle, tittle-tattle,
Babble, rabble, gnash and nibble
Hiss and distant windy whistle
Suck and sigh and sexy sidle
Crackle snap of apple fire
Squeaky scrunch of steps in snow
Fizz and sizzle, roar and rumble
Creaky cackle, thumping thunder
Whiney whisper, lilting lisp
Hum and jingle, jangle bang
Throaty trumpet, tooting youth
Shrieking silence, hush your mouth.

Sinister Christmas

He's gauche,
a leftie and wrapping paper
does not cooperate.
The colourful rolls wrestle,
conspiring secretly
to unroll when he least expects it.

Scissors, stubborn in his
gawky grip, revolt.
The tape gives viscous kisses
where it shouldn't
and won't stick where he wants.

The festive corners are not crisp,
the paper-wastage appalling
but he tries again
and again
until the pile is complete
and I promise
next year
we'll use cloth bags instead.

Lunatic Love

We watch the moon rise
naked over island hills,
a scarlet woman unashamed.
She sails more flagrant with each sigh
past puritan clouds
that aim to shroud the demimonde.
On this bright night
our naked limbs twine white
in the glow of her cameo shoulders,
our smiles slow as hers.

Incandescent,
she pauses behind trees
standing in silhouette
outside the open blinds;
a pale audience
to our own erotic dance.

Passionate parentheses, your hands
trace my face and neck.
"Swan"
You smile and hold me
featherless.
The moon slips from our window,
a silver spy spiriting her secrets
towards the day.

At dawn still we lie,
you smiling sweetly asleep,
your eyes track dream-deer
and flutter on stolen wings.
Stripes of Venetian sun
stir you awake and we move
together once more.

Lost

The desert
I must cross
to reach you
gets wider
every day.
No oasis to offer
hope or soften
the harshness of this
journey
only I must make.

Behind me, footsteps come
from a place
we both have made.
Before me, on the next
wave, a shimmering
mirage of what you
used to be. If I strain
to hold you, keep you
with me, the mirage melts
leaving me
weeping at the insult.

You are the innocent
smiling with no
recognition. I too am
sinless, mourning
the loss of the living
and dying of thirst

www.ingramcontent.com/pod-product-compliance
Lightning Source LLC
LaVergne TN
LVHW041642060526
838200LV00040B/1680